Alfred's INSTRUMENTAL CD+ INSIDE PLAY-ALONG

Tenor Saxophone

Easy Instrumental Solos f[or]

Special Occasions & Celebrations

MW00666910

Contents

Title	Occasion	Month	Page	mp3 CD Track Demo	mp3 CD Track Play-Along
Tuning Note (B♭ Concert)					1
Auld Lang Syne	New Year's Day	January	3	2	3
We Shall Overcome	Martin Luther King, Jr. Day	January	5	4	5
She Loves You	Valentine's Day	February	7	6	7
Danny Boy (Londonderry Air)	St. Patrick's Day	March	9	8	9
The Irish Washer Woman	St. Patrick's Day	March	11	10	11
I'd Like to Teach the World to Sing	Earth Day	April	13	12	13
Because He Lives	Easter	April	15	14	15
Peter Cottontail	Easter	April	17	16	17
Cielito Lindo	Cinco de Mayo	May	18	18	19
A Mother's Prayer	Mother's Day	May	21	20	21
You Raise Me Up	Father's Day	June	23	22	23
Trumpet Tune	Weddings	June	25	24	25
Pomp and Circumstance	Graduations	June	27	26	27
America the Beautiful	Independence Day (4th of July)	July	29	28	29
Summertime (from *Porgy and Bess*)	Summer	August	31	30	31
This Land Is Your Land	Labor Day	September	32	32	33
The Chicken Dance (Dance Little Bird)	Octoberfest	October	33	34	35
Funeral March of a Marionette	Halloween	October	35	36	37
Come Ye Thankful People, Come	Thanksgiving	November	37	38	39
Away in a Manger (Medley)	Christmas	December	38	40	41
Jingle Bells	Christmas	December	41	42	43
You're a Mean One, Mr. Grinch (from *How the Grinch Stole Christmas*)	Christmas	December	43	44	45
I Have a Little Dreidel	Hanukkah	December	45	46	47
Happy Birthday to You	Birthdays	All	47	48	49

Arranged by Bill Galliford, Ethan Neuburg, and David Pugh.
Recordings produced by Dan Warner, Doug Emery, Lee Levin, Bill Galliford, and Ethan Neuburg.

Alfred

Alfred Music
P.O. Box 10003
Van Nuys, CA 91410-0003
alfred.com

ISBN-10: 1-4706-1921-0
ISBN-13: 978-1-4706-1921-3

Alfred Cares. Contents printed on 100% recycled paper.

Track 2: Demo
Track 3: Play-Along

AULD LANG SYNE

Words by
ROBERT BURNS

Traditional Carol

WE SHALL OVERCOME

Track 4: Demo
Track 5: Play-Along

Adaptation by
GUY CARAWAN, FRANK HAMILTON,
ZILPHIA HORTON and PETE SEEGER

Moderately slow (♩ = 88)

SHE LOVES YOU

Track 6: Demo
Track 7: Play-Along

Words and Music by
JOHN LENNON and PAUL McCARTNEY

Bright rock (♩ = 152)

Track 8: Demo
Track 9: Play-Along

DANNY BOY (LONDONDERRY AIR)

Words by
FREDERIC WEATHERLY

Traditional Irish Aire

Slowly (♩ = 72)

THE IRISH WASHERWOMAN

Track 10: Demo
Track 11: Play-Along

Traditional Irish Folk Song

Irish jig (♩. = 86)

I'D LIKE TO TEACH THE WORLD TO SING

Words and Music by
BILL BACKER, ROQUEL DAVIS,
ROGER COOK and ROGER GREENAWAY

Track 12: Demo
Track 13: Play-Along

Track 14: Demo
Track 15: Play-Along

BECAUSE HE LIVES

Words by
WILLIAM J. and GLORIA GAITHER

Music by
WILLIAM J. GAITHER

*A♯ = B♭

PETER COTTONTAIL

Track 16: Demo
Track 17: Play-Along

Words and Music by
JACK ROLLINS and STEVE NELSON

CIELITO LINDO

Track 18: Demo
Track 19: Play-Along

Traditional Mexican Song

45
mf
61
f
1.
2.

A MOTHER'S PRAYER

Track 20: Demo
Track 21: Play-Along

Words and Music by
DAVID FOSTER and CAROLE BAYER SAGER

YOU RAISE ME UP

Track 22: Demo
Track 23: Play-Along

Words and Music by
ROLF LOVLAND and BRENDAN GRAHAM

TRUMPET TUNE

Track 24: Demo
Track 25: Play-Along

Composed by
HENRY PURCELL

POMP AND CIRCUMSTANCE

Track 26: Demo
Track 27: Play-Along

Composed by
SIR EDWARD ELGAR

AMERICA THE BEAUTIFUL

Track 28: Demo
Track 29: Play-Along

Words and Music by
SAMUEL WARD

Moderately slow (♩ = 88)

SUMMERTIME

(from *Porgy and Bess*)

Track 30: Demo
Track 31: Play-Along

Music and Lyrics by
GEORGE GERSHWIN,
DuBOSE and DOROTHY HEYWARD
and IRA GERSHWIN

Slowly (♩ = 80)

THIS LAND IS YOUR LAND

Track 32: Demo
Track 33: Play-Along

Words and Music by
WOODY GUTHRIE

THE CHICKEN DANCE (DANCE LITTLE BIRD)

Track 34: Demo
Track 35: Play-Along

Music by
TERRY RENDALL and
WERNER THOMAS

FUNERAL MARCH OF A MARIONETTE

Track 36: Demo
Track 37: Play-Along

Composed by
CHARLES GOUNOD

*A♯ = B♭

Track 38: Demo
Track 39: Play-Along

COME, YE THANKFUL PEOPLE, COME

Words by
HENRY ALFORD

Music by
GEORGE J. ELVEY

AWAY IN A MANGER (MEDLEY)

Track 40: Demo
Track 41: Play-Along

Music by
JAMES R. MURRAY (1887) and
WILLIAM J. KIRKPATRICK

45
8
54
p
mf
mp
70
rit.
p

JINGLE BELLS

Track 42: Demo
Track 43: Play-Along

Words and Music by
JAMES PIERPONT

Moderately fast (♩ = 144)
(𝅗𝅥 = 72 This represents the song pulse feel counted in two.)

YOU'RE A MEAN ONE, MR. GRINCH

(from *How the Grinch Stole Christmas*)

Track 44: Demo
Track 45: Play-Along

Lyrics by
DR. SEUSS

Music by
ALBERT HAGUE

I HAVE A LITTLE DREIDEL

Track 46: Demo
Track 47: Play-Along

Traditional Hanukkah

Moderately bright (♩ = 144)

HAPPY BIRTHDAY TO YOU

Track 48: Demo
Track 49: Play-Along

Words and Music by
MILDRED J. HILL and PATTY S. HILL

PARTS OF A TENOR SAXOPHONE AND FINGERING CHART

When there are two fingerings given for a note use the first one unless the alternate fingering is suggested.

When two enharmonic notes are given together (F♯ and G♭ for example), they sound the same pitch and are played the same way.

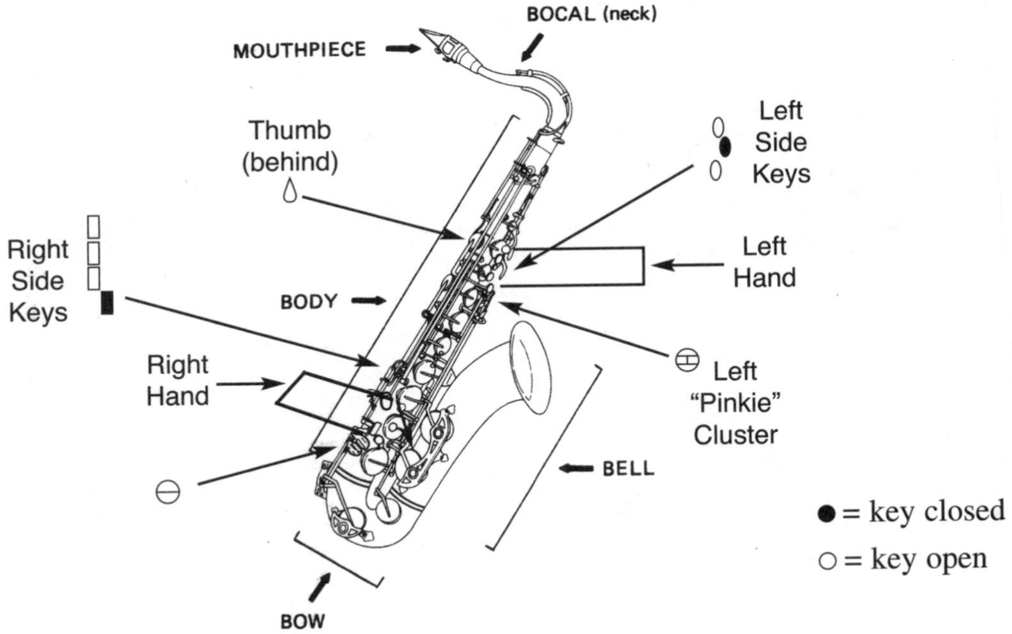

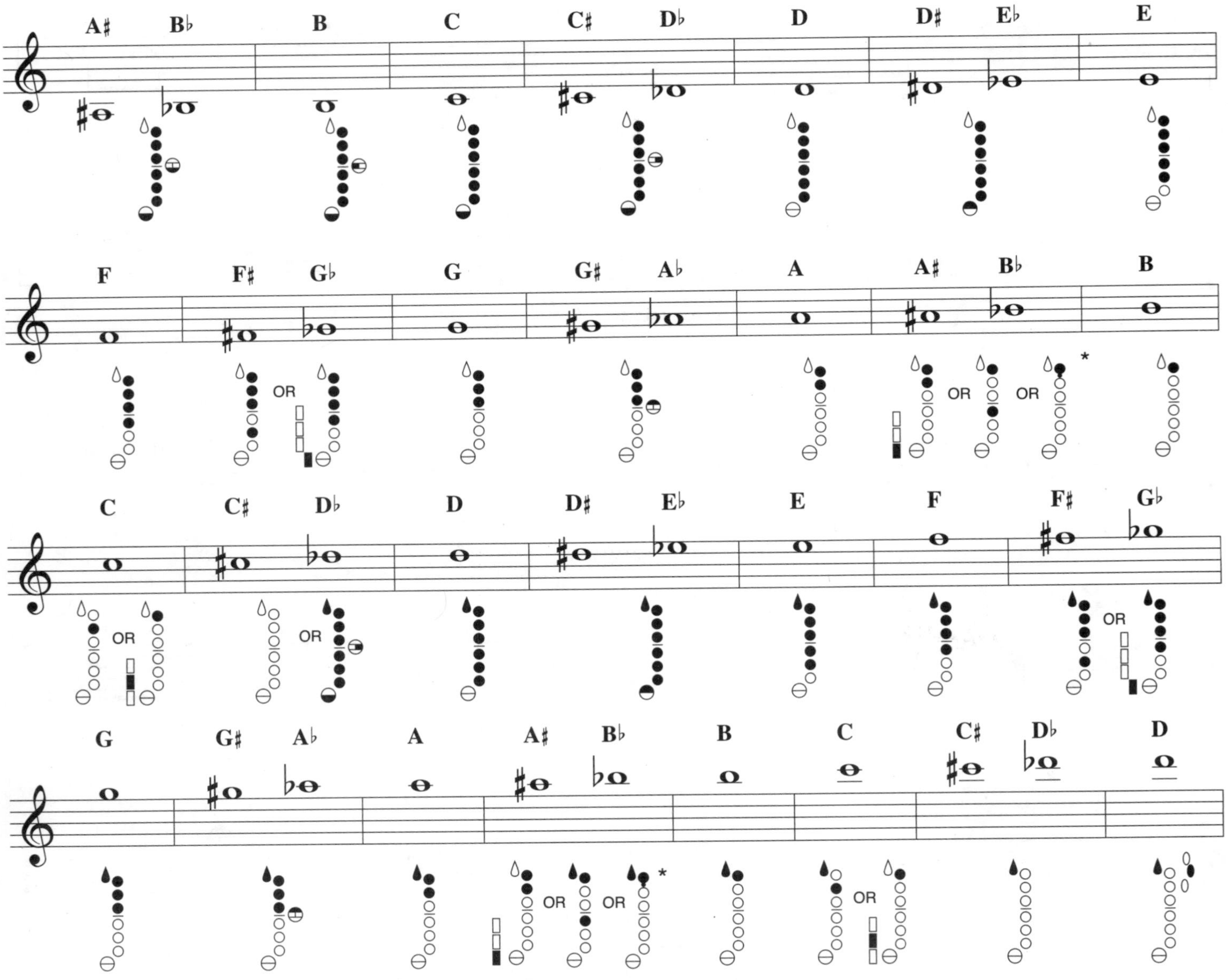

* Both pearl keys are pressed with left hand 1st finger.